Rescued Set Free

Delivered From D[illegible] A[illegible] Death

Lesley-Jane Mcnally

Editing, cover design and author services by Opulent Books: www.OpulentBooks.net

ISBN: 978-1-916691-39-1

Dedication

Lord Jesus Christ, my eternal guide and source of strength.

Acknowledgements

I am grateful to our Lord Jesus Christ, Our Heavenly Father, and the Holy Spirit for accompanying me throughout my journey and never abandoning me. Glory be to God.

I want to extend my heartfelt thanks to Joe Benjamin for his professional and compassionate guidance and patience as a mentor for the book.

I am deeply thankful to my daughter Jade, whose unwavering support has sustained me through my trials. Her bravery and courage in her own journey have been a great source of inspiration to me.

I wish to acknowledge Jenny Weaver for her assistance in propelling me forward and enabling me to walk in the Spirit.

Table of Contents

Preface

This is my narrative of redemption and forgiveness, a true chronicle of spiritual warfare and triumph. Growing up, the concept of spiritual battles eluded me until much later in life. Led astray onto dark paths, I found myself in the grip of evil forces during my darkest moments.

Yet, in the middle of the torment, I discovered a Saviour powerful enough to deliver me from the clutches of destruction.

This book may startle some; it is intended for the sceptics and the disbelievers, aiming to unveil the truth and illuminate the path towards an intimate relationship with God. It explores His character, His boundless love for His people, and

His relentless pursuit of reconciliation.

I learned that life, is not merely physical but profoundly spiritual. Many remain unaware, walking with veiled eyes, oblivious to the spiritual forces shaping their struggles. The passage from below underscores this reality, reminding us of the unseen battle raging in heavenly realms.

Finally, my brethren, be strong in the Lord, and in the power of his might. Put on the whole armour of God, that ye may be able to stand against the wiles of the devil. For we wrestle not against flesh and blood, but against principalities, against powers, against the rulers of the darkness of this world, against spiritual wickedness in high places.

Ephesians 6:10-12 (KJV)

Amidst this earths conflict for souls, discovering the truth empowers us to stand firm and overcome. It grants us the loving shelter of our Creator, liberating us from the enemy's grasp. The journey to freedom is one guided by the Word of God, where His mercy and grace abound, offering forgiveness for our transgressions.

Even in Satan's futile attempts to hinder this book's publication by trying to scam my money online. His efforts pale in comparison to the power of God. For Christians, death holds no fear; it is merely a transition into eternal glory. This narrative stands as a testimony to the grace of God in my life.

Chapter 1

The First Encounter with Darkness and Abandonment

In received a prophetic message concerning Revelation 12:4 from an Apostle of Christ. Prior to that, the Holy Spirit had already revealed it to me personally, helping me understand the reasons behind the attacks I faced.

And his tail drew the third part of the stars of heaven, and did cast them to the earth: and the dragon stood before the woman who was ready to be delivered, for to devour her child as soon as it was born. Revelation 12:4 (KJV)

Growing up in London, England, to a working-class family with Mum, Dad, and two siblings in a three-bedroom maisonette, life seemed ordinary. Our holidays were enjoyable, and my parents seemed content. My relationship with my elder siblings appeared strong, being the youngest of three.

Sharing a room with my sister, we had twin beds on opposite sides, with walls adorned with pop idols from the 70s and psychedelic duvet covers, typical of the era. Unaware of the challenges awaiting me, I was a shy and sensitive soul.

One night, while in bed, I turned over and was struck with horror as I saw an old lady looking down at me, her face covered in warts. I screamed, fleeing to snuggle between Mum and Dad. I recounted seeing the terrifying old lady, but Mum assumed it was a nightmare. However, for me, it felt very real.

Little did I know, this was only the beginning of the spiritual warfare that would unfold in my life. By the age of eleven, my parents' relationship had deteriorated, with my father involved in an affair before eventually leaving us all. This left Mum heartbroken and struggling financially to raise us.

I took his departure particularly hard, often sobbing into my pillow at night and praying for his return. The person I once saw as a pillar of strength and the source of joy in our family had abandoned us for the allure of temptation. His new partner, a ten years younger slim blonde, exacerbated the pain, as he made no effort to maintain contact with us after leaving. I mourned not only the loss of a father but also the loss of a selfish one.

In later years, my father revealed that I was an unplanned child (and I believed I suffered womb rejection), a revelation that shed light on my early struggles with self-worth, anxiety, and dysfunctional attachments. These issues manifested in various ways, from avoidance and trust issues to feelings of inadequacy and loneliness in relationships.

The wounds inflicted on my soul ran deep and

would profoundly affect my future relationships with men, far beyond what I initially realised. Meanwhile, my father remained distant, building a new life for himself, remarried, and starting another family.

I picked up the broken pieces of myself and threw myself into following a boy band to distract myself in the early 70s. I went into rebellion, and with no one to discipline me, my mum showered me with love while I roamed aimlessly, trying to mask my pain.

Despite my own struggles, I also did what I could to support and comfort Mum. Witnessing her tears and her turning to drink took a toll on the family, but fortunately, she managed to pull herself out of that dark place. She displayed remarkable inner strength and resilience, forced to put on a brave face and rebuild our lives single-handedly.

Meanwhile, Dad remained noticeably absent. We were essentially sidelined when my step-sister came into the picture. It was particularly tough because whenever my father called, he'd gush about her, oblivious to how it made us feel. I felt rejected to my very core.

Starting secondary school at age eleven, I struggled to fit in. I endured severe bullying from a classmate who even had the audacity to pull our teacher around by her hair. The school environment became terrifying, leading me to skip classes frequently to escape the torment. Eventually, I was placed in a special unit and escorted off the school premises for my safety, allowing me to focus on my studies. At this point, I grew indifferent towards many people, finding solace in my own company. So at this young age, I was battling through a living hell – bullied and emotionally scarred by my parents' divorce, with my mind in turmoil and no counselling to guide me.

I remember stumbling upon a Ouija board in our family home, bewildered by its presence and unsure of its purpose or origin.

At the tender age of sixteen, I was out at a

discotheque with friends dancing and enjoying music. This had a huge well-being effect and I was starting to heal inside and on the other hand, my mum was dating and happy again.

I met David a young man who was two years older than me. I was smitten and we became friends and then love took over. I was young, naïve and desperate for acceptance. I went on the pill behind my mum's back and had sexual relations with him. I was obsessed with him and unfortunately, he became my focus. After we started dating I found out he had a dark side. He would steal cars and was always in trouble with law enforcement. On top of that, he was also dating another girl at the same time as me.

I was suffering from rejection from my father and when your father can't show love towards you, then I was keen to receive acceptance from Men, even if they were not good for me. Desperation was fuelling my need for love and acceptance.

My heart was once again shattered by his

unfaithfulness to me. I resolved not to let him slip away and endeavoured to secure his exclusivity, yet he remained indifferent to the pain he caused, oscillating between me and her. I spent countless hours in tears at home, longing for his return and for him to forsake her. My mother was deeply distressed to witness my shattered state, compounding my feelings of worthlessness and rejection.

Eventually, he left her behind, and we became engaged to be married. I was wed at eighteen, and shortly after that, my son arrived at the tender age of nineteen. We secured our first home together in a London flat near Big Ben.

Several years passed, and all seemed well on the surface. Then, by chance, I stumbled upon pornography when I discovered his hidden VHS tape. Curiosity led me to insert it into the video player one day while he was out, and I witnessed my first pornographic film. I was astounded. How could people display their intimate acts on screen? And why was he indulging in this within our marriage? We had exchanged vows before God at our wedding – what was this betrayal? Feeling shocked and disheartened, I chose to keep my discovery to myself, fearing it would lead to our separation. Yet, I knew it would gnaw at me, for our values clearly diverged. Who was this man? The echoes of abandonment and rejection from my father reverberated early on, as my self-esteem plummeted. Clearly, I needed to embark on a journey of self-discovery.

As time passed, my husband's behaviour turned abusive, culminating one day when he pinned me against the wall, his hands around my throat. I knew I needed an escape.

Recognising the mental, emotional, and spiritual abuse, I initiated divorce proceedings. We parted ways, and I found myself alone at home with my son. His father failed to honour his promises to spend weekends with him, leaving me stranded on street corners with the pram. Frustrated, I issued an ultimatum: consistency or absence. I yearned for my son to have a steadfast, loving father, but he failed to meet that standard. History was repeating itself in the life of my child.

Chapter 2

Unlawful Entry Into My World

My mum continued to be my pillar of strength as my son Jamie and I went through life alone. He attended school while I juggled a part-time job.

I ventured into dating again, but none of the relationships blossomed. I was testing the waters, hoping to find acceptance despite being a broken and rejected child, plagued by a sense of worthlessness. As a single parent, I grappled with insecurity, especially since many girls my age were childless. I realised my reactions were rooted in trauma from earlier years, as the Lord revealed after salvation. This drove me to strive harder to attract boys my age – not in a promiscuous manner, but by exemplifying kindness and authenticity. I was merely twenty-one when my divorce was finalised.

At twenty-four, my beloved Nan fell ill. She was ninety-three, and her presence meant the world to me. Standing steadfast by my mum's side, we faced the inevitable as Nan was admitted to the hospital with pneumonia and eventually passed away.

Then came the unexpected twist. After Nan's demise, my mum disclosed something startling – a medium who purportedly communicated with the departed. Intrigued, I allowed my curiosity to lead me, and Mum arranged for us to meet a local woman named Mrs Blake, a renowned spiritualist medium.

In hindsight, I wish I had possessed more wisdom, but I was naive and unaware of what lay ahead. Stepping into the spirit mediums room, I sat eagerly awaiting a message from my late Nan, oblivious to the deceit being woven into my impressionable heart. At that moment, I lacked any frame of reference or truth to guide me.

Regard not them that have familiar spirits, neither seek after wizards, to be defiled by them: I am the LORD your God.

Leviticus 19:31 (KJV)

The Mental Hospital

One evening, I was at home with my son, tucking myself up in bed. Suddenly, I felt a heavy presence envelop me, pinning me down to the bed. I struggled to open my eyes, hearing voices around me as if there were people in the room. Despite my efforts, I remained paralysed from head to foot, unable to see what was happening. Slowly, the oppressive presence lifted, and I jolted upright, switching on the lamp beside me. What had just occurred left me utterly bewildered.

I kept the light on, unable to shake off the sheer horror of the experience, traumatised and fearful.

Should I dare to close my eyes again, for fear of a recurrence? I pondered over the question, eventually drifting off to sleep.

The following day, I sought comfort in visiting my mum and recounted the disturbing events of the previous night. She dismissed it as nonsense, refusing to entertain any further discussion on the matter. Little did I know, this was merely the beginning of demonic manifestations in my life.

For weeks, I grappled with recurring episodes of sleep paralysis and unsettling voices. The pinnacle of terror came one night when I felt my body lift off the bed, witnessing myself tossed about like a rag doll by unseen forces. Overwhelmed and terrified, I reached a breaking point, dialling my mum at 2 am and hastily deciding to seek refuge at her place with my son. Hastily, I called for a cab and left my flat in a frantic rush.

Escaping My Haunted Home

The notion of summoning a vicar for an exorcism crossed my mind, but then another idea emerged – to seek help from the spiritualist church. Perhaps my mind was so consumed by torment and confusion.

After enduring six weeks of nightly terrors, my mum insisted I visit the doctor. Reluctantly, I agreed, and we arranged an appointment.

Arriving at the doctor's office, I felt a surge of nerves, unsure of what his response would be. After my name was called by the receptionist, I knocked on the door and entered, greeted by the familiar face of my doctor, who had known me since birth.

He extended his hand and gently asked, "So tell me, Lesley, what's been happening to you?"

I began recounting the unsettling experiences, unaware of the spiritual battle unfolding for my soul. While I had a belief in God, He lingered somewhere in the recesses of my mind, a distant memory from my days in Sunday school at age six.

"Thank you for confiding in me," he said reassuringly. "I'm going to give you a letter. I want you to go to St George's, a psychiatric hospital nearby, with this letter. Today."

His sense of urgency was palpable, though I remained oblivious to the supernatural aspect of my plight. Grateful for his guidance, I accepted the letter and left, consumed by anxiety.

Upon arrival at the hospital, I was met by a nurse who took my details and suggested I stay the night. I was taken aback. "Why?" I questioned.

"Just for observation," she replied calmly.

Trusting her judgment, I followed her to the ward. In a stark room with large windows, I found myself alongside a woman with anorexia, the two of us isolated from the rest of the hospital.

Donning oversized pyjamas and a dressing gown, I settled in for the night, while my mum, back at home with my son Jamie, fretted over my well-being.

I pondered to myself how the events unfolding at my flat back home could be observed from this hospital, yet the presence of darkness manifested once more.

Attempting to engage in conversation with the lady in the adjacent bed proved fruitless; she remained withdrawn and visibly nervous, so I respected her space.

Around 9 pm, as I settled into sleep, a hissing sound filled the air. I glanced up to witness a colossal snake in an unsettling vision slithering towards me on the hospital floor. In a frenzy of fear, I leapt from my bed, screaming for assistance and pleading for my mum's presence. Overwhelmed and terrified, I realised my reactions were rooted in trauma from earlier years.

Traumatic experiences can serve as gateways for oppression and torment, a reality evident in many mental health institutions. Whether the abuse is emotional, physical, sexual, or verbal, its impact is profound. I sought solace in keeping busy, grateful I never turned to drink or drugs, for which I thank God.

The nurse swiftly administered a sedative,

urging me to ingest it for calmness. Succumbing to its effects, I drifted into a sedated slumber, with the nurse vigilantly by my side. Reflecting on this episode, I realised that God allowed the enemy's influence to prompt me to seek divine protection – a realisation that strengthened my faith.

The following morning, I found myself in a room surrounded by psychiatrists and trainee doctors, under the guidance of an elderly physician. He diagnosed my experiences as hypnagogic hallucinations, attributing them to blood rushing to my head while lying down – a scientific explanation for what I believed to be supernatural encounters.

Despite the medical diagnosis, I remained steadfast in my belief that these encounters were indeed supernatural. The doctor prescribed tranquillisers and scheduled a follow-up appointment in a month's time.

Grateful for divine intervention, I recognised the enemy's schemes to confine me to the institution, hindering me from fulfilling God's will.

Reflecting on the power of faith, I realised the vulnerability that comes from acknowledging God without understanding the role of Jesus Christ in our lives. God, I realised, is not only a loving presence but also a protective shield against the devices of Satan.

Chapter 3

Wrong Place Wrong Time

The day I left the hospital, I collected my medication from the chemist and visited Mum, who was overjoyed by the diagnosis. We embraced warmly before Jamie and I returned home, carrying on with our routine.

Strangely, I experienced no further episodes of nighttime paralysis or hearing voices. As I diligently took my medication, I began contemplating the need for spiritual protection.

One day, while in my kitchen, a sudden sharp pain shot through my lower back, causing my knees to buckle beneath me like jelly. I collapsed to the floor, calling out for assistance as I struggled to rise. After a while, I managed to stand and rested, later realising that it was a fiery dart from the enemy, as revealed to me by the Lord after salvation.

I began praying at home, seeking an angelic presence to guide and protect me. Researching online, I stumbled upon information about Archangel Michael and his reputed divine protection. Despite my disillusionment, I sought advice about my recent experiences. However, influenced by my newfound beliefs in New Age philosophy, I chose to attend a spiritualist church, believing the falsehood that I could communicate with the departed – a notion that took root in my consciousness.

Now the Spirit speaketh expressly, that in the latter times some shall depart from the faith, giving heed to seducing spirits, and doctrines of devils; 1 Timothy 4:1 (KJV)

I sought healing from a practitioner named John. Upon entering his room adorned with Native

American pictures and talismans, he claimed that his deceased son served as his guide in providing healings. As I lay on his couch, enveloped in a blanket while calming music played, I inexplicably grew freezing cold. For thirty agonising minutes, he laid his hands on me, unknowingly welcoming demonic influence into my life.

Feeling deceived and desperate for guidance, I requested to speak with a church leader. I was seeing in the spirit, and a door had been opened to the spiritual realm via trauma. The woman I confided in dismissed my concerns, insisting that my experiences were a gift and offered protection. Despite her explanation, I expressed my fear and discomfort, vehemently rejecting this so-called gift and pleading for its removal. Though she argued the benefits, I remained steadfast in my unease. Later in life, I realised that all healing came from God alone. I was young and naïve then and had not yet seen a Bible.

Who his own self bare our sins in his own body on the tree, that we, being dead to sins, should

live unto righteousness: by whose stripes ye were healed. 1 Peter 2:24 (KJV)

As humans, we embrace the illusion of our own power, yet all authority emanates from Above rather than below. Later, I discovered that God gives gifts to His children, including the gift of healing. However, I also learned of a counterfeit spirit in the world, manipulated by the disobedient.

Believing I possessed such abilities, I delved deeper out of curiosity. I began attending a church hosting Mediumship evenings, longing for messages of hope from departed loved ones. My worldview expanded with New Age ideologies and teachings. Eager to explore healing, I enrolled in a Reiki Level 1 course after seeing an advertisement. Once certified, I eagerly offered to help my mother, who was suffering from a painful knee. Guided by my training, I laid my hands upon her, and within twenty minutes, she walked without pain or limp. Both astonished, we pondered the possibilities ahead.

With a natural inclination towards helping others, I contemplated the potential of this newfound gift. I pursued extensive training, eventually becoming a certified Angelic Reiki master/teacher. My journey led me to invest heavily in courses on alternative healing, tarot, angel card readings, and massage therapy, plunging deeper into the realm of esoteric knowledge. I started going down this dark rabbit hole!

I was consumed by thoughts of my future and the need to assert control and find solace. Obsessively, I turned to daily horoscopes, making it a ritual to read my stars in every newspaper I could find. It became a compulsion I couldn't resist. In my state of confusion and despair, I felt utterly lost and broken.

Be sober, be vigilant; because your adversary the devil, as a roaring lion, walketh about, seeking whom he may devour: Whom resist stedfast in the faith, knowing that the same afflictions are accomplished in your brethren that are in the world. 1 Peter 5:8-9 (KJV)

My sister, too, grappled with life's challenges and sought help from alternative healers, eventually becoming a massage therapist.

Above all, I yearned for peace and tranquility, my spirit wounded and fractured. I embarked on a quest for truth, yet found no solace in the world. Questions plagued me: Was there existence beyond death? Could we attain healing through chakra balancing? What was the significance of the ubiquitous Kundalini practices?

Enticed by these mysteries, I explored various avenues, succumbing to the allure of psychic fairs offering alternative remedies. The world seemed to offer an abundance of paths towards healing, a goal I fervently pursued to overcome trauma and abandonment.

Experimenting with Kundalini yoga, I unwittingly invited further spiritual turmoil into my life. Unaware of our divine creation by God, even my childhood exposure to Sunday school left me with scant recollection at the tender age of seven.

I knew the Lord's Prayer from school and needed it badly. I did not think to use it because what was about to happen was going to take me to another level in demonic activity that I could not have known if I had no Bible to rescue me.

And God said, Let us make man in our image, after our likeness: and let them have dominion over the fish of the sea, and over the fowl of the air, and over the cattle, and over all the earth, and over every creeping thing that creepeth upon the earth. So God created man in his own image, in the image of God created he him; male and female created he them.

Genesis 1:26-27 (KJV)

Chakra healing became an integral aspect of my life, leading me to delve into numerous books on the subject. Rooted in Indian philosophy, it posits the existence of energy centres within the body, the blockage of which can precipitate illness. I would often close my eyes, visualising a cleansing process akin to scrubbing a soiled saucepan, all in pursuit of the belief that self-healing is attainable through focused thoughts.

My curiosity extended to the base of the spine, purportedly the locus where the awakening of divine femininity and the wellspring of sexual energy occurs. The underlying premise was to attain empowerment, seize control of one's life, and foster stability and grounding in the world.

However, my subsequent discovery revealed a darker truth: this practice serves as a gateway for the python spirit to enter. The symbolism of Kundalini, represented by a snake spiralling upwards from the base of the spine to the crown of the head in pursuit of enlightenment, explains the deception that ensnared me.

Following my engagement with yoga, I

experienced intense sexual impulses, ensnared by a spirit of lust. Yoga, with its spiritual openness, lacked the protective hedge, leaving me vulnerable to such demonic influences – lust embodied by the snake symbol.

As I practiced, my body would oscillate between sensations of heat and cold, accompanied by tremors. Misled by the rhetoric of New Age practitioners, I interpreted these sensations as manifestations of energy – positive or negative. My heightened state of awareness fostered a deeper connection to the spiritual realm, unwittingly granting Satan access to my spirit.

Unaware of Satan's influence at the time, I remained deceived, a plight shared by many who remain ignorant of this reality.

Introduction To Another World

Several months later, while visiting my sister, she suggested meeting her friend Hazel for lunch. Eager for the company, I gladly accepted. Over lunch, our conversation veered towards my newfound interests, prompting Hazel to divulge her own experiences. She recounted her husband's battle with multiple sclerosis and his encounter with a vicar who prayed in tongues – a concept unfamiliar to me. Hazel advocated for seeking God through meditation, urging me to abandon my practices.

Despite her counsel, which lacked mention of obtaining a Bible, I embraced the idea of quieting my racing thoughts and finding solace in solitude. Thus, the following week, I retreated to my bed, seeking to still my mind and relax in quiet mediation.

This Book of the Law shall not depart from your mouth, but you shall meditate on it day and night, so that you may be careful to do according to all that is written in it. For then you will make your way prosperous, and then you will have good success. Joshua 1:8 (ESV)

We are meant to fill our mind with scripture not empty it.

I drifted off to sleep during my attempts at meditation, finding it increasingly alluring. With each session, I began experiencing vivid visions. A piercing eye bore into my consciousness, and soon, I found myself glimpsing future events. Thrilled by this newfound ability, I felt a sense of mastery over my destiny. Eager to go deeper, I summoned angels to accompany me, yearning to connect with my supposed guardian angel and uncover her name – an entity I believed to be assigned to each of us from birth.

Unbeknown to me, these encounters were orchestrated by familiar spirits, gradually entangling me further in deception.

The newfound practice of meditation offered a dual purpose: relaxation and a quest for divine protection, spurred by Hazel's assertion that God could be found through meditation. Unwittingly, I opened myself up to familiar spirits masked as my guardian angel, even assigning her a name. With each session, I sought solace in this imagined presence, unaware of the sinister deception at play.

In my ignorance of traditional avenues of seeking God – such as attending church or consulting the Bible – I unwittingly stumbled deeper into deception. My naivety, rather than leading to enlightenment, only served to further entrench me in spiritual peril.

Driven by a desire to seize control of my life and alleviate the suffering I keenly felt within, I grappled with existential questions of identity and purpose. My fascination with the angelic realm led me to immerse myself in the study of angels, eventually becoming an angel teacher under the guidance of a worldly mentor. Inadvertently, I found myself leading others astray, perpetuating the cycle of deception.

But seek ye first the kingdom of God, and his righteousness; and all these things shall be added unto you. Matthew 6:33 (KJV)

Chapter 4

The Angel Rescue

It was just another day, and I found myself shuffling my cards, but an overwhelming sense of dread washed over me as I laid out the spread. The cards seemed to foretell a grim future, filled with death, despair, and pain. Regretfully, I wished I had never looked, yet the accuracy of these readings always troubled me deeply.

I was on my way to London to meet my friend Sarah for the Notting Hill Carnival – a vibrant celebration of culture and music that has been a staple since 1966. Sarah and I had been friends since secondary school, bonded by our shared birthday and mutual fondness. As I journeyed on the train towards her home, an inexplicable unease settled over me. Upon arriving at the station, I couldn't shake the feeling of heaviness in the air as I navigated through the bustling streets of London.

Upon reaching Sarah's flat, the atmosphere was jovial as we shared coffee with her friends. However, as we made our way towards the carnival, a sense of apprehension gnawed at me. The streets were crowded, and I felt a palpable tension in the air, exacerbated by the sight of individuals concealing their faces with hoodies.

Suddenly, a strong presence gripped my right arm, accompanied by a vivid white light in my mind's eye. Despite my attempts to shake it off, it clung to me like an invisible weight. Overwhelmed by fear, I abruptly excused myself and retreated to the safety of Sarah's flat. Yet, once inside, I felt compelled to open the window – a strange urge I couldn't comprehend.

As I struggled with the window, a force seemed

to yank me away, propelling me towards my friend's bed. To my astonishment, the words "Saved by an angel" materialised on the wall before me, sending shivers down my spine. Terrified, I hastily gathered my belongings and fled to the nearest train station, consumed by the urgency of escape.

Upon returning home, I recounted the harrowing experience to Sarah, attributing it to a divine encounter with an angelic presence. The following day, as I sought solace in church, I was confronted with yet another sign – an unmistakable title, "Saved by an Angel" by Glennyces Eckersley, resting on a chair between myself and another parishioner.

Reflecting on the events of that fateful day, I couldn't ignore the chilling synchronicities that unfolded. The card reading, though ominous, had unwittingly foreshadowed my deliverance from harm. The area's reputation for crime and drug activity hinted at the presence of territorial demons, bent on wreaking havoc.

Seeking counsel from a trusted friend – a police officer – shed light on a sobering truth: a woman had tragically jumped from her window during the carnival, mirroring my inexplicable urge to do so. In that moment, I realised the gravity of divine intervention and the protection afforded by angelic guardians.

Though I had yet to fully embrace salvation, I found consolation in the knowledge that even in my disobedience, God had not forsaken me. In my darkest hour, I had been watched over and spared from the clutches of darkness. And so, with newfound reverence, I continued to call upon the Archangel Michael for advice guidance and Archangel Raphael healing, acknowledging their presence in my journey towards redemption.

For he shall give his angels charge over thee, to keep thee in all thy ways. Psalm 91:11 (KJV)

Chapter 5

Another Marriage

When I was 25, I began going out to clubs again with friends while Mum looked after Jamie. I was desperate to have some fun, to let music and dancing lift my spirits. I was driving at the time, so I always used that as an excuse not to get drunk. I hated drinking; I simply loved music and felt that alcohol was dangerous, seeing many young women fall into a stupor, leaving themselves vulnerable. I had a strong sense of needing to keep safe.

I met my second husband at a club, and once again, I was swept away by his gentle voice. I tried to get his attention by chatting with him, hanging around him, and building a friendship first.

To my shock, I discovered that he was engaged to another lady, and I felt as if the same thing was happening again.

I was upset, but I still tried to get his attention. One day, I heard they had split, so I spent more time with him. Eventually, we started dating. My single parent status made me try too hard to earn his affection. The root issue was abandonment, although I was not aware of what was driving me to distraction. I wanted him to be with me, and it happened. By the time I was 29, I was married to him, and another child came along, my daughter. We started a family life, and he proved to be a good man who accepted my son as well.

Despite my insecurities, I tried to be a good wife, cooking the best food and waiting on him hand and foot. I was loyal and never looked at another man. He was quiet in nature, nothing like my first husband, and we both worked.

We managed to buy a house, which was great news – a place with our own garden and a three-bedroom semi in a lovely suburb. What more could I ask for? The house was a mess and run down; it was going to take time and money. I started working long hours to pay the bills, but with a young baby, I found myself overstretched.

Simon was drinking and falling asleep a lot on the sofa. I developed postnatal depression and had a nervous breakdown at the age of 32, leading to antidepressant medication. Some days, I was in a daze, not knowing what I was doing. The wedge between us widened into a chasm. I began hating myself for not feeling settled inside. I was a mess, a broken pot needing to be put back together, but I didn't know how.

I started hating life in the world. Why was there so much suffering? Why was I constantly getting into wrong relationships? So, with two children aged 3 and 15, I was alone.

I sought advice from a psychic reader and also sat with my angels in despair, feeling alone, and experiencing more rejection. I cried many days and nights, wondering why life was so cruel to me. I fell into self-pity mode and had to find a way to pull myself out of this pit somehow.

When my daughter started school, I joined a diving club. I had a need for adventure and escape; I wanted to be still in nature, away from the noise and busyness of life. Underwater was the place to be. My diving holidays helped me relax; when I was with the fish and amazing coral, I would wander off into my own world. I was becoming a dreamer; I wanted to know why life was not as I expected it to be. I had fantasies of happy-ever-afters, but reality was different.

Ironically, one of the Tarot cards had 'the World' in it. If you got this in a reading, it was a good sign; it meant that you would gain success in the world – money, love, career, family – all perfect as one would expect. However, I saw how this was all empty; nothing in this world could fill this void. Something was missing big time, but I had not worked it out quite yet.

Matthew 4:8 (NIV) reads, "Again, the devil took Him up on an exceedingly high mountain, and showed Him all the kingdoms of the world and their glory."

But worldly things did nothing for me. I was not materialistic; I was spiritual and kind-hearted, with a heart for the needy and weak. Yet, I was already lost, broken, and bemused by this world's view of happiness.

John 16:33(NIV) says, "I have told you these things, so that in me you may have peace. In this world you will have trouble. But take heart! I have overcome the world.

I was in the world lost.

Whom was my identity in? The world or the spirit inside of me?

I started to try to find myself. I helped people as much as I could, and spending time alone was good for me to heal and find some peace again. I started a business in outside catering, delving into my passion for cookery. I cooked for weddings and found myself in the funeral business, catering for the bereaved and providing support to family members, believing that angels were around them. I was always on the lookout for feathers as a sign of an angel's presence.

Years went by, and I was offered a contract at a health club. I was excited to be earning a good wage, as the franchise was a busy one. As I sat in the room preparing for the interview to win the contract, I saw a brick wall in my inner vision, blocking the kitchen door like a 'no entry' sign. This made me think, 'Oh, my angels are trying to tell me I won't get this job.' I was upset because I wanted it badly; it was going to open a door to financial freedom, and I wanted to give my children a decent life. However, I ignored the signs and hoped and prayed for me to get this contract.

Eventually, I did get the contract, but still, an uneasiness lingered within me, and I had no idea why. I wanted to distance myself from the New Age stuff and try again. Weeks went by, and I received the news that I'd won the deal and was to take on this busy health club food/bar. I was confident it would be great. However, the guy who was leaving did not tell me the truth regarding its monthly income. I gave up my outside business to immerse myself in a job from hell.

The guy left, and because I did not buy his china from him, he sabotaged the beer pumps and reset the till, causing further problems.

Maybe the angels were trying to warn me with the brick wall at the door, saying 'don't go in there,' but it was not clear. I read it as 'I would not get it,' and I was determined too. I had no choice but to get stuck in and make this work, overcoming the traps he had set for me. I soldiered on and changed the menu, getting my family to help out, mainly Mum acting as a deputy manager in my absences. It was full-on 24/7.

I began to see I had bitten off more than I could chew, and days turned into nights. It was all a blur from one week to the next, with food orders, beer orders, staff rotas, staff holidays, etc. Wow, I was earning my money alright. I was carrying a weight I never knew I had with all the emotional turmoil in my past. I kept myself busy to stop myself from thinking about it all, I guess.

The clients were not that nice, adding more problems. They started to pick on small things not right in their sight. Wow, it was all getting too much. My father suggested I get a friend of his to do a stock check and see if the money was tallying up each month. David, his name was, was a tall man who struck me first and was good at his job.

David turned out to be good with the money. He noticed a shortfall in the takings and was to hit me with it. We sat down over a coffee, and he said the beer money is out. He suggested that some beer was being given away for free to the local guys attending the gym, and I had my suspicions it was the barman. As I could not be there each night, we left him in charge.

I had to suspend Malcolm and get a new barman in ASAP. One morning, I was near the bar, and a lady had walked down the stairs that led to the pool area. There was a ledge near the staircase where I left my briefcase. It was a very wide ledge. I heard a scream and went to see what happened. My briefcase had been moved and fell on her head. Not only this, but it was the worst customer who loved to complain a lot.

All hell broke out then. My name was in the club owner's office as being negligent and causing her to have this accident. Thankfully, I was not near the briefcase at the time, and witnesses were there to prove my innocence. But I was more concerned about how it was tipped off the ledge, which was wide. I felt there was some supernatural force behind this. I was perplexed and upset. It was getting worse day by day.

The day came when I had a meeting, and I decided to quit this place and gave my notice into management after 9 months of hell. Sadly, I was £17,000 down in takings as well. Later in life, I was to realise the python spirit was behind this loss. I ignored the warning signs from God and hence paid the price. I had to remortgage my home and pay off the debt to the taxman.

The thief cometh not, but for to steal, and to kill, and to destroy: I am come that they might have life, and that they might have it more abundantly. John 10:10 (KJV)

Chapter 6

The Church Lady

After leaving the health club, I found myself at home, striving to make ends meet while occasionally venturing out. Thankfully, I never harboured a desire to drink, which served as a blessing amidst the trials I had already endured. There seemed to be an inner resilience propelling me forward into a new chapter.

For ten years, I sustained myself by conducting New Age courses and offering card readings from the comfort of my home, content in my solitude and busyness. One solitary evening, as I sat at home, two candlesticks inexplicably tumbled off the fireplace, and the fridge emitted strange noises, sending shivers down my spine. Spooked by these occurrences, I resolved to visit a Baptist church the following day.

At the church, I encountered a gracious Chinese lady who welcomed me warmly. In conversation, I confided in her about the eerie incidents in my home and my reliance on card readings for daily guidance. Unperturbed, she suggested visiting me the next day to discuss matters further.

True to her word, she arrived punctually the next morning, and over tea, we delved into discussions about God's love and His desire for us to join Him in heaven after death. As she led me in prayer, I hesitantly voiced my thoughts aloud, feeling unsure about addressing an unseen entity. Yet, she assured me that God hears our prayers.

Inviting me to her home for lunch, she endeavoured to keep me in her company, offering prayers on my behalf. Gradually, she broached the subject of the cards I used, cautioning me about their potential harm and God's disapproval. Although she refrained from mentioning the Devil initially, she later warned me about the consequences of not following God and Jesus, including the prospect of hell.

This revelation instilled fear in me, prompting questions about God's love and His intentions. Though she provided me with a tract, she omitted to give me a Bible. Despite attending church a few more times, I grappled with the notion of hell, feeling as though I was being manipulated, especially when she hinted at my mother's potential damnation.

Regrettably, I chose to distance myself, succumbing to naivety and deception, ultimately rejecting the messenger sent by God to guide me and my family. Little did I know, this decision would lead me down a path of further hardship and spiritual disarray, wandering aimlessly without a shepherd.

Then when lust hath conceived, it bringeth forth sin: and sin, when it is finished, bringeth forth death. James 1:15 (KJV)

I began to grow apprehensive about what I perceived as brainwashing, although she never directed me to the chapter regarding divination. Many years of sorrow could have been spared.

There shall not be found among you any one that maketh his son or his daughter to pass through the fire, or that useth divination, or an observer of times, or an enchanter, or a witch. Or a charmer, or a consulter with familiar spirits, or a wizard, or a necromancer. For all that do these things are an abomination unto the Lord: and because of these abominations the Lord thy God doth drive them out from before thee. Deuteronomy 18:10-12 (KJV)

My life resembled the book of Job; Satan was unleashed, and I remained ignorant of the Bible.

But every man is tempted, when he is drawn away of his own lust, and enticed.

James 1:14 (KJV)

Soon after I arrived at the diving club to enjoy a weekend away, I found one of the guys there. I found one of the guys to be calm and gentle in nature, unlike the brash types I never liked. His name was Simon. We would have social nights, gathering together many evenings in the clubhouse, with lots of drinks flowing, and some indulging in soft drugs, and Simon was part of this circle. I recall witnessing cheating among married men, affairs that deeply upset me, and feeling sorrow for the wives at home. Stripper nights and such events made my spirit uneasy. By then, I believe I understood why it troubled me, what turmoil was stirring within. One night, a lady scheduled for a striptease had her car break down, resulting in the cancellation of the event. I felt relieved and happy.

The place where I sought rest and enjoyed scuba diving was alive with fornication, drunkenness, adultery, and various sins. Simon and I began dating, with him often drinking while I observed, occasionally joining in but regretting it the next day, vowing not to get drunk again.

I met his parents, who lived in Kent. They too enjoyed drinking wine and gin, often evident during our visits. Feeling like the odd one out, as I preferred sobriety, I listened to stories of Simon's drunken nights, and how his parents used to rescue him from park benches after he was overcome with beer. Despite these revealing signs, I ignored the red flags, always seeking companionship and undervaluing my self-worth, unwilling to wait for a partner who lived a life free from drugs, alcohol, and perversion.

We enjoyed diving trips overseas, but I noticed Simon distancing himself from the others. An awkward situation arose as he struggled between his old habits and his new life with me. He understood my disinterest in the drunken, drug-filled nights they once enjoyed while away.

At the age of 41, we tied the knot at a Turkish resort with a celebrant, rather than in a traditional ceremony before God. We then relocated to Kent, where I owned a house and he had a flat. Despite being nine years younger than me, and despite my awareness of his drinking issues, I chose to turn a blind eye to the red flags.

My decision to move upset my mother, who resided in Surrey, although my sister was nearby for support. As we settled into our new home, we gradually distanced ourselves from the dive club where we had first met. Our activities shifted to walking holidays and other leisure pursuits. While he remained reserved on some days, making conversation difficult, he continued to indulge in alcohol while I remained sober.

Living with us at the time was my daughter, who didn't warm up to my new lover. She preferred to retreat to her room, creating tension in the household. Despite this, my daughter maintained regular contact with her father, and he and I spent most weekends together. He accepted my Reiki healing work and other New Age therapies I conducted from home, as I preferred to maintain a work-life balance by working from home and taking care of household responsibilities.

My husband would often go out with his work friends on Fridays and return home late, leaving me with an uneasy feeling. Despite my concerns, I chose to accept his behaviour and carry on with our life together.

Another Strange Encounter

One night, while lying alone in my bed, I witnessed books flying off the shelf and crashing onto the floor, followed by a picture near my bedside shattering as it plummeted to the ground. Feeling alarmed, I instinctively called upon Archangel Michael for assistance, unaware that I had left a door open to the enemy at that time.

My lack of understanding about what was happening stemmed from my naivety, ultimately putting me in a vulnerable position. I used to attribute people's unpleasant behaviour or aggression to mere bad energy or vibes, oblivious to the fact that demons could be influencing their motives.

Dealing With Pornography Again

Years passed, and during a cookery weekend in Somerset, a feeling prompted me to return home earlier than planned. Upon arriving home, an impulse led me to the computer where I discovered pornography flagged up on the internet. Disturbed by this finding, I called my daughter into the room and questioned her about it. She assured me it wasn't her doing.

Determined to get to the bottom of it, I went into the search history and uncovered evidence of pornography being watched on the computer. Shocked and incensed, I confronted my husband about it when he emerged from the bathroom. Despite his denial, righteous indignation surged within me, and I was overcome with anger, contemplating drastic actions like throwing the computer out of the window.

But I say unto you, That whosoever looketh on a woman to lust after her hath committed adultery with her already in his heart.

Matthew 5:28 (KJV)

Do you remember when Jesus overturned the tables in the Temple, enraged by the moneylenders conducting business? Well, I felt a similar fury within me, for deep down, I felt a profound sadness for those ensnared in pornography, especially the children – a sense of injustice gripped my soul. It was unlike my usual peace-loving self. In a fit of rage, I removed my wedding ring and stormed out of the house with my child. I felt deserving of loyalty in every form, refusing to tolerate such evil around me. This surge of hatred towards pornography was unfamiliar but consuming.

He was visibly shaken; he had never witnessed this side of me before, and my face contorted with anger. I stayed away, grappling with where to go and what to do. I felt a mix of emotions – sadness, betrayal, confusion, and intense anger. A few days later, after I had calmed down, I returned home. At that time, I didn't think I knew God; I only called upon angels for comfort.

I confronted him about his actions and poured out my heart to him. Over the years, I persevered, enduring various challenges. One night, Simon, in his drunken state, began slandering my daughter, unjustly. Despite my inner turmoil, I had to endure – it was my third marriage, and I felt compelled to continue.

Six years later, one fateful night, I received a call from my husband at 1 am. He was incoherent, claiming he had been put into a police van and had no recollection of how he got there. Concerned, I agreed to meet him at the train station. His face was bloodied, resembling that of a war casualty. Shocked and bewildered, I rushed him to the hospital for treatment. He claimed to have walked into a lamppost, but my intuition told me otherwise. His condition, worsened by alcohol, left me feeling broken and helpless. I cried out to the angels for protection as I realised I had married an alcoholic and a porn addict, plunging my life into further despair.

At 47, I received the devastating news from my

brother: my mum had passed away. My world shattered in an instant – she was my rock, my guiding light, the epitome of a wonderful mother.

The shock was overwhelming. I was prescribed anti-depressants and diazepam to cope with the despair. Writing this now, tears flow as God heals yet another layer of my pain.

That event pushed me to the brink. I felt an intense urge to break free from the worldly life I was living, to let go. I remember pleading with the Angels, desperately begging for this cycle to end. Collapsing onto my bed, tears streaming, I couldn't bear the thought of enduring it all over again.

The shame of past failed marriages weighed heavily on me; I couldn't fathom another one going awry. Yet, a deep inner voice urged me to surrender, to find strength in letting go. Looking back, I see how God was shaping me, pruning away my self-reliance and worldly desires.

In my pursuit of love, security, wealth, and home, I sought them from others rather than from the One who provides all good things. It wasn't until I went into the Word of God that I began to understand. Like peeling layers of an onion, God revealed my true identity in Him – I was discovering who I was in Christ.

It became increasingly apparent that there was a pervasive darkness ensnaring him and entangling me in its deception. However, within me, the Spirit of God stirred, discerning that something was amiss.

Be ye not unequally yoked together with unbelievers: for what fellowship hath righteousness with unrighteousness? and what communion hath light with darkness?

2 Corinthians 6:14 (KJV)

Chapter 7

The Warfare Commences

After the breakdown of my marriage and feeling deeply upset, I faced the prospect of losing my home and all my wealth. With insufficient income to pay the mortgage, surrendering became inevitable. Amidst this turmoil, my children remained my source of strength. I continually sought protection, clinging to whatever provided me solace. Thoughts of suicide crossed my mind as a means to escape the internal pain, though the notion felt selfish considering my children. Despite feeling lonely, I persevered, recognising the need to break free from cyclical patterns. It was time to cease circling the same mountain.

But thou, O Lord, art a God full of compassion, and gracious, longsuffering, and plenteous in mercy and truth.
Psalm 86:15 (KJV)

I was upset because so many people were destroying others' lives. I thought there is more to life than money. I had a deep sense of humanity in my soul and wanted to serve in some way, to make a difference.

Yea doubtless, and I count all things but loss for the excellency of the knowledge of Christ Jesus my Lord: for whom I have suffered the loss of all things, and do count them but dung, that I may win Christ.

Philippians 3:8 (KJV)

I was given a new home from a charity, and it meant all I had longed for was taken away from me:

a husband and a house with a garden. I had nothing that I wanted, like most people in the world; I desired a steady life. The first day I was to view my new home with two bedrooms, I looked on the floor, and a rainbow appeared. I felt that was a sign from my angels, and a smile came on my face again.

Around 2017, I was having trouble with my back. I was in severe pain and could not feel my bladder or my feet. I went to the GP, and he advised me to get to King's College as soon as possible – no going home, no driving. So, I did just that, and I was rushed into the hospital with Cauda Equina, a condition that can cause paralysis. I had urgent surgery on my lower back. The years ahead were to be the start of my health deteriorating. Some days, I could hardly walk and was in and out of the hospital with slipped discs.

The MRI showed all my bones were dry in my spine, and the slightest exercise in the gym would cause the discs to bulge and intense pain. There were many hospital admissions and weeks in hospital beds because I could not even walk. I had rehab, but I had to resort to just swimming. I used to love exercise; it gave me some good endorphins. Years of sorrow and suffering had hit my health.

A merry heart doeth good like a medicine: but a broken spirit drieth the bones.

Proverbs 17:22 (KJV)

So I went about my business of teaching healing and found myself employed as a telephone reader on the psychic phone lines, using angel oracle cards and my intuition to help people. Many would call me in pain and sorrow, and I felt compelled to offer some hope. I was pouring out my love on others but actually needed to keep some for myself.

This provided me with income, freedom, and time to meditate alone and stay connected to the Angels. At this stage, I had no idea that God had a plan to save me from deception. With no other source of income, my classes were popular, and my website attracted many people who liked the idea of angel healing and empowerment. My business was called "The Angels Within."

One day, an American lady from Sweden called me for a reading. She seemed pleasant enough with a sweet voice, and we became friends. She showed me her deck of cards, which were very gothic and dark with images of dragons and witches. I felt uneasy inside.

I visited her home in another country and attended her wedding. While lost in her town, she was with her father at the hotel suite. Eventually finding her home, I noticed all the curtains were drawn, and it felt dark and eerie inside. My spirit did not like it, but I settled down and got some sleep. The next day, I attended the wedding and was relieved to return home soon after, catching a flight back to the United Kingdom.

A few weeks later, she called me in a bad mood on a video call. She said she was doing Angel readings online, and a guy had upset her, so she showed me a doll and claimed she had put a hex on him. The doll had ropes around it. My spirit was filled with fear, and I tried to calm her down. I realised she was not on my page. I questioned myself, "Why are you doing this?" This felt like witchcraft.

Soon after the call ended, I called on Archangel Michael to come to me and protect me. I saw a different side to her, and it was my first encounter with a dark witch. I questioned myself, "What was I doing? Why am I attracting this into my life?"

Weeks went by, and she continued to call me. At this point, I was scared to upset her, so I found myself treading on eggshells. She insisted on coming to see me for a long weekend. I had no idea how to stop this.

When she arrived in the United Kingdom, we went to Glastonbury, a pagan town in Somerset, full of New Age shops with crystals and some Wiccan shops, which repelled me. I preferred the Angelic stuff over the Wiccan religion. As we approached the hotel front, a few steps up, a grass snake slithered past me. I felt uneasy; something wasn't right.

As the night went on, we sat and talked in the

hotel gardens and then retired to the room. Soon after, as I was sitting on my bed, a sharp stabbing pain came over my arm, and I screamed in agony. She showed no interest in my pain or its cause. When it stopped, she started attacking my beliefs, saying things like "you and your Angels, your light and fairy stuff," but I calmly explained why I liked the Angels.

She then disclosed that she suffered from bipolar disorder. I showed sympathy towards her and kept the conversation away from New Age beliefs. I wanted the weekend to end; I think she could sense my fear. I felt her dark presence and prayed for protection.

After dropping her at the airport, a sense of ease came over me. We didn't speak much after that weekend. Looking back, I think she was sent to harm me.

As the weeks went by, strange things started happening in my home. A chair fell over in front of me as I walked past the dining table, causing me to trip and fall on my shoulder, which later caused much pain and a frozen shoulder. Then, a few weeks later, a large mirror in my bathroom behind the toilet came crashing down on the floor just in time for me to miss it.

I knew someone was doing something to me, so I prayed and cried out to the angels to protect me. Despite these incidents, I didn't stop teaching or doing readings.

At one point, I did wonder why people did not ask God for guidance and instead asked Angels, but it was a temporary fleeting thought, and I dismissed it. My home had a table in the lounge adorned with images of Ascended Masters, Angels of the Bible, and Jesus, amongst them carrying a lamb. I also had a crucifix with Him on it, as I thought this would protect me. I had allowed Satan access to me, and he was starting to try to destroy me: failed relationships, accidents, financial loss, homelessness. Yet, I never gave up hope for life to be better. I was following the cards in front of me, made by the devil, to lead people away from the truth. How naive was I? But God was faithful and never let me be destroyed totally. Looking back, I can relate my life to the book of Job.

The stalker was next to come and attack me. Another agent was sent, this time disguised as a student who wanted to learn healing. I had no idea at the time, but I was giving readings to an American guy who was expressing violent intentions towards his girlfriend. He was angry and aggressive, and I became afraid to take his calls, so I blocked them. Then he started emailing me, displaying a sense of urgency and dominance. He became obsessed with trying to reach me.

This strange guy signed up for Angelic Reiki in London with two other ladies. I felt the need to call him and get his address, so I rang him, but he did not answer. Two weeks later, I asked him for his address to send him the receipt for the Reiki course. Some wisdom was coming to me to be prudent. He gave me his address in London, and I sent the receipt as promised. Exactly two weeks before the course was due, I had a spine issue and was rushed into the hospital. This turned out to be divine intervention and protection.

Feeling worried about teaching in a few weeks' time from my hospital bed, I had to ring the students, hoping they would reschedule with me. I had taken a £52 deposit from each of them, and I hoped it would not upset them. How wrong was I? When I rang him, he was furious. He had an outburst of anger and slandered me over the phone. I explained that I was bedridden and unable to walk, but he was unrelenting.

For he shall give his angels charge over thee, to keep thee in all thy ways.

Psalm 91:11 (KJV)

The next few days were a nightmare as I lay in my hospital bed, in pain and stitches, a myriad of abuse flooded my mobile device. Messages accusing me of being scum, needing to be stopped, demanding the return of money, all from the man who was supposed to be interested in healing others, showing no act of gentleness towards another human being! I replied, promising to refund his money once I was out of the hospital. However, something in my spirit warned me, and I decided to call the police.

I informed the ladies about the cancellation of the weekend and expressed my fear from my hospital bed. After spending five days in the hospital, I had to go to my father's home to rest and recover. During this time, a total of 54 threatening and abusive text messages flooded my phone. He also attacked my social media pages, defiling my name.

Upon finding his Facebook page, I discovered that he had shut it down. The enemy was attacking my livelihood, and I had to take down my website out of fear of running workshops in case he turned up. In hindsight, I saw God's hand on my life, as I asked if this was the same guy from America who had come to England to stalk me, and I received confirmation. The angry American was after me too; he had previously mentioned visiting the United Kingdom.

Upon returning home to my safe space, I received a call from the police. They arranged a visit to my home, where I showed them the address he had given me and all the threatening texts. I explained how I couldn't earn money and had to start all over again.

They said they would visit his address in London and trace his number. However, the address turned out to be fake, just like the person himself, who was attempting to attend my healing weekend. The Crown Prosecution Service was to deal with it, and the police took over the case. They mentioned that his phone was the only hope to trace him via the provider, but it would take some time.

Weeks went by, and I found myself having to rethink my life. The only income I had was from telephone calls now, and I hated it. While I initially believed I was helping people with counselling and advice, it was draining me of my energy. I questioned how I ended up in this situation. My ego was in control, and I enjoyed the positive comments I received from people about how good and accurate I was. The encouragement kept me going, even though I had no idea it was demonically inspired and driven.

I was deeply deceived and needed to find a way out. After a month or so, I received a call from the police stating they were not going to proceed with my case since he had not messaged me for a while. This was a bombshell, and I felt incredibly upset and let down. How could someone destroy my livelihood and get away with it? I felt that God was not pleased with me for being in deception, but I needed His word to show me that I was indeed deceived.

Now the works of the flesh are manifest, which are these; Adultery, fornication, uncleanness, lasciviousness, Idolatry, witchcraft, hatred, variance, emulations, wrath, strife, seditions, heresies, Envyings, murders, drunkenness, revellings, and such like: of the which I tell you before, as I have also told you in time past, that they which do such things shall not inherit the kingdom of God. Galatians 5:19-21 (KJV)

When all the dust had settled, I carried on, desperately longing to find a job outside of the house and to break free from the new age nonsense. I persisted, trying self-employment and various jobs to escape this work, but none brought me the needed income. Financially, I could never seem to level up or break through. I spent thousands training in different areas, yet I always found myself back at home, earning money from telephone calls.

One night, as I slept, I felt a huge python slither up the side of my body, over my head, and down the other side. Frozen in fear, I realised I was truly trapped by this python, wreaking havoc on my life. In hindsight, I couldn't understand why I never ran to a church. It seems crazy now. I didn't grasp the significance of the snake encounter and didn't realise it was the enemy. I was unaware of the demonic kingdom and its hierarchy, having unknowingly given it access through going to a medium with my mum and experiencing trauma from abandonment. I hadn't recognised that life is spiritual and we are in the flesh.

It's important to remember that the Holy Spirit and the python spirit are not equal adversaries of good versus bad. The python spirit is a defeated minion of the enemy with limited power, and it has no power unless you give it to him. It simply masquerades as a powerful force, catching people unaware and chipping away at what the Holy Spirit provides: the breath and freedom of the Lord.

I wasn't free yet, but by grace, I was saved, as you will see later on in this book.

Finally, my brethren, be strong in the Lord, and in the power of his might. Put on the whole armour of God, that ye may be able to stand against the wiles of the devil. For we wrestle not against flesh and blood, but against principalities, against powers, against the rulers of the darkness of this world, against spiritual wickedness in high places. Wherefore take unto you the whole armour of God, that ye may be able to withstand in the evil day, and having done all, to stand. Stand therefore, having your loins girt about with truth, and

having on the breastplate of righteousness; And your feet shod with the preparation of the gospel of peace; Above all, taking the shield of faith, wherewith ye shall be able to quench all the fiery darts of the wicked. And take the helmet of salvation, and the sword of the Spirit, which is the word of God: Praying always with all prayer and supplication in the Spirit, and watching thereunto with all perseverance and supplication for all saints.

Ephesians 6:10-18 (KJV)

After all the trauma with those people, I decided I needed a break. So, I booked myself a retreat to detox in the Spanish mountains. I flew out in June, eager to detox, but little did I know it would involve a week-long fast with only liquid and juice.

Upon arrival, I met other people, and it was truly a treat. The atmosphere was calm and peaceful, and the scenery was heavenly. This was shaping up to be a good week to shed some weight. The retreat offered yoga, and I participated in an hour of it each day, spending the rest of my time relaxing by the pool.

One day, my curiosity led me to a lady offering foot massages, so I booked an hour with her. It turned out to be quite interesting. As I entered the room, I met a tall African lady. As I lay on the bed, she started talking to me about my feet, noting that one was rigid and advising me to relax more. She asked me questions about my life as she rubbed my feet. As I relaxed further and did some breathing exercises, she asked, "What do you see?" I replied, "The colour yellow." Then she asked, "And what else do you see?" I responded, "Jesus."

After the session, I was bewildered. Upon reflection, I realised that the Lord was trying to approach me during the fast, using this retreat in Spain as a means to relax me. Yet, I still did not search for God; I was focused solely on Archangel Michael.

Despite all the chaos and deception, Jesus would appear to me in dreams before my salvation. He showed himself on a mountain many times, but I never fully understood the Bible or the word of God at that time.

Chapter 8

Father Healing And Jades Cancer

I was now living alone after the last incident with the stalker, and I became fearful of life. I had no desire to be in a 9-5 job because I cherished the freedom to carry out what I called counselling and to be where I needed to be. I enjoyed the Angel groups I used to run; they were very popular. Additionally, I had some magazine interviews about my Angelic encounters, and this media coverage drew people to me. I aspired to be known in the world as the "angel lady" with books in bookstores. I had big plans for my work to achieve worldwide success. But God had other plans.

I enjoyed going out in my local area and meeting new people, as well as attending my Jive nights. I loved dancing; it made me happy.

I had been estranged from my father for 10 years. I told him in a letter that he was not a good father, and I expressed how I felt he was selfish and greedy. I had to let it all out; it was all in my heart.

Ten years passed, and I was invited to a family wedding. Myself and my daughter attended, as my son was out enjoying life. It was there, standing in the sunshine, that I spotted my father with his wife. I felt awkward, knowing I had written my truth in that letter. I chose to ignore him and prayed for protection.

However, he came over and said, "You are my child. I want to make amends with you." He started chatting, and I sensed his awkwardness. He said, "I can't just stand here with my daughter and grandchild in the distance." I felt he was being convicted of his pride. We sat down, and he spoke some hard truths. I never knew God had planned this, as what transpired some 10 years later was amazing.

We began seeing each other again, and we put the past behind us. He started inviting us over to his house, but I noticed some tension with my stepsister. She had seen the letter I wrote all those years ago, and she was mentioned in it. However, being a peacekeeper, I let it all go.

What I noticed in my father's house was a lot of idols. He had Egyptian paintings everywhere, statues made of stone of Roman gods in his garden, and figures of Neptune and other Roman gods. I had no idea this was idolatry, as I did not have a Bible to see the truth.

I started dating again, yet still felt insecure and alone. The natural human desire to be loved never left me, and I held onto hope.

Many years passed, and I found myself feeling stuck, far away from the rest of my family, as if I had been abandoned. I tried to build a life for myself.

My daughter became independent and left home, leaving me feeling lonely.

Then, one day in 2016, while I was at home, a picture of my daughter kept falling off the windowsill. I found it strange. Every time I put it back, it fell again. It felt as if someone was trying to get my attention regarding my daughter.

She was living in Somerset with her partner, leading a life similar to mine. What happened next hit me hard. I received a call from my son, informing me that he wanted to see me and that they were driving over from Surrey. I lived in Kent. I wondered what this visit was about.

Three family members arrived, and my son sat me down. He explained that Jade had been in a car accident. Thankfully, she was okay, but during her hospital examination, they discovered a cyst on her brain. My world collapsed around me, and I burst into tears, crying out for my baby.

They said they wanted me to go back with them to my son's home, and we were going to drive to

Somerset the next day to see her, so we all went to Jamie's. My daughter was still in the hospital. How much more can a woman take? I thought one thing after another kept going wrong.

Upon arriving in Somerset and entering her home, I found many family members already there, including Jade's father and his wife. When I saw Jade, she looked so thin. I hugged her tightly, unable to hold back the tears.

We all gathered in the lounge, and they sat me down to tell me the truth. While my son had initially mentioned it was a cyst on her brain causing the seizure, her stepmother revealed that Jade had a brain tumor. I cried uncontrollably. They informed us that she would be seeing a cancer specialist after her scan to discuss the diagnosis.

This was going to be another week away, so I stayed the night at Jade's home. At this point, I took Jade upstairs and retrieved some Angel cards from my bag, praying for hope. The cards I laid out indicated that healing was coming; they did not suggest death. However, she wasn't keen on seeing them, and she didn't want Billy, her boyfriend, to see either. He showed no interest in my Angel work and clearly wasn't fond of me. I noticed his cannabis tray in the house, indicating his drug use, which troubled me deeply. I expressed my concern to Jade, with a tone in my voice.

Be not deceived: evil communications corrupt good manners. 1 Corinthians 15:33 (KJV)

I left several candles around the house, each with Angel messages of peace and hope. I couldn't deny my identity as someone who sought to heal; everyone knew about my interest in health and healing. That night, I cried myself to sleep in her spare room, feeling a deep pain in my heart.

The next day, I was reluctant to leave her; I just wanted to be by her side. However, she lived three hours away, and the family wanted to take me back home. So, after the longest week, we returned to Jade's home in the country, ready to meet with the cancer nurse for the diagnosis. When she arrived and sat down, chills ran over me. She delivered the news that Jade had a large tumour on her brain that required urgent surgery for removal. Everything was happening quickly to give her a chance.

Knowing there were different types of cancer, some more dangerous than others, I pulled the nurse aside before she left and asked in a weak, afraid tone, "It's not malignant, is it? Please say it isn't." I desperately hoped she would say it was benign, but she explained that they couldn't determine that until the surgery was done and the tumour tested in the lab. Fear, grief, anger, and a tidal wave of sadness engulfed my spirit. I wanted her to reassure me, but she couldn't say a thing.

After she left, I fell apart, crying uncontrollably. I retreated to the garden with other family members and hid in the toilet, crying away from Jade so as not to upset her. It was a dark moment, and I couldn't understand why this was happening to us. We were kind people.

Again, I had to go back that night, leaving Jade,

and this upset me deeply. She was very much in love with this guy and hoped to have a future with him. However, thank God that never happened because what transpired over the weeks ahead revealed his true identity.

We received a date for the operation and booked into the hospital accommodation. Jade had an entourage of 10 family members, all encouraging her and lifting her up. She was only 25, just a baby. Walking into the hospital with a blanket over her head, she was trying to be strong. I had to wait 12 hours for the results as she underwent 12 hours of brain surgery to remove the large lump in her brain. It was the longest day of my life.

I went off to the Somerset town to meet some spiritual friends and be with them in their beautiful garden. At 5 PM, I received a call from the surgeon saying that everything went well and they had managed to remove most of the tumor. I jumped for joy. He explained that it was a grade 2 Astrocytoma, a slow-growing cancer that had likely been there for years until it outgrew her brain cavity, leading to the seizure. However, they couldn't remove all of it. I arranged to meet with him the next day.

All I wanted to do was hug Jade and reassure her. When I arrived back at the hospital, I sat with her. She had a huge scar that reached behind her ear, and her head was stitched up with metal staples. I tried to stay strong in front of her.

The next day, we saw the occupational therapist, who was there to help her regain her brain function. The therapist brought over some puzzles and animals, like what a 2-year-old would recognise. Jade's face was partially paralyzed, and she had difficulty guessing the animals to test her cognitive skills. She got many wrong; for example, she mistook a giraffe for an elephant and struggled with basic knowledge.

I was shocked. It was clear that it would take time for her memory to come back, as the tumor had affected that area of her brain.

I was in such despair seeing her life change overnight. Within three days, she was eager to leave the hospital, and this became the next challenge the enemy had planned for me. She returned to her boyfriend's mother's house as I lived far away. I had no chance to care for her, and she couldn't eat or drink much, reliant on others. My caring spirit just needed to be there for her, and I felt wrenched inside.

Back home, I had no choice but to leave my child in the hands of another woman. My relationship with Jade's boyfriend was about to be tested. I tried calling Jade on her phone and his, to no avail. When he did answer, he claimed she was always sleeping. I didn't believe him and kept asking for a call from my child. But a week went by with no contact, and my rants to family yielded no joy.

Feeling desperate, I called a psychic who mentioned the Devil card appearing among others with swords. I knew then that swords represented the tongue. He was up to his tricks again. After two weeks, I'd had enough of the game-playing and decided to show up unannounced. Not having any contact with Jade after such a major operation tore me apart, and righteous anger rose within me.

As I prepared to stay in a Bed and Breakfast near their home, everything was arranged. On the motorway, a huge truck in front of me had a large Tasmanian Devil cartoon with the words "hands off, she's mine." It felt like a sign urging me to rescue my daughter from this relationship, showing he was a control freak.

Arriving at the gate, their shocked faces greeted me. I confidently asked to see Jade. The house was set out with a large side garden near the front door, and as I glanced over, I saw my child under a canopy with a recliner chair, wrapped in a blanket. My heart sank to see her weak and suffering. I went straight to her, and she asked why I was there. I explained that I couldn't reach her and decided to visit, all the while smiling, knowing their evil plan to keep me away from my sick child had backfired.

Whoso diggeth a pit shall fall therein: and he that rolleth a stone, it will return upon him. Proverbs 26:27 (KJV)

Jade was shocked at my boldness, and it took her a while to relax. When they went inside to gossip about me, I told her that Billy didn't let me speak with her, and I was upset. She said she had been tired but that's all, and she was getting her strength back, but she looked wiped out and weary.

I sat with her and gave her some gifts, trying to hold back the tears. The mother was sneaky and off in her approach; it was clear they were scheming behind my back. Even though I hadn't met her much before Jade's diagnosis, he was clinging to his mum all smug.

When I had to leave, I decided not to stay in the town but to drive home again. Jade promised me she would call me. She stayed in touch with me, and as months went by, he became distant from her, perhaps because he knew she had a cancer condition that couldn't be completely removed surgically. She started to call me as he was out in the pub some nights; she was lonely, and the cracks were appearing in her relationship.

She called me, saying she wanted to come home back to her family and live. She missed her family, and we made plans for her to move on and start again. He had caused her a lot of pain with his aloofness. By January of the next year, she was back with me, and I cuddled her in my arms as she wept openly.

Jade's cancer started to grow back later, and the cavity in her brain filled with water. They had to operate again and put a stent in, like internal plumbing leading down to her stomach so all the fluid could drain off. Another time of worry and despair came when she had to have her chemo to stop the growth from coming back again. This was six weeks of intense radiotherapy, and her hair fell out. I was upset but strong; where I got my strength, I don't know. The chemotherapy was to follow, but first, her eggs had to be frozen in London, at a specialist hospital for cancer patients who were young enough to have children still.

I remember when Jade was at home one night in her mobile home, the Lord gave me a vision of his hands over her head; he was standing by her bed. This filled me with faith.

While Jade was going through treatments, she started to live and work on a farm looking after dogs. She was tired a lot, and it took all her strength to do it. Her brain needed simple things as it was too much for the remaining tumor was still causing blurred vision. It was going to be a long road to recovery. But after Jesus appeared, I knew it was going to be okay. I had still not been saved at this point in 2018.

I was moved from my home through a home transfer via my housing company, ending up back near my family, which was a miracle as I couldn't see a way to move home.

Shortly after my home move, I applied for Jade to be moved nearer her family, and God moved for her. She was given a one-bedroom flat just one mile away from me, so I could take over a caring role, helping her with daily things. We were settled again and near each other. Looking back, I could see God had a plan, and what was to happen was beyond a miracle.

Chapter 9

The Man With The Addiction

I was settling into my new home, reflecting on how lucky I was to be back in my hometown after 15 years in another part of the country, a move I regretted when I was 41. Living alone, I began to explore local groups and activities, joining Meetup for evening meals and walks around town.

During one of these meals, I spotted a guy who looked very familiar. As we chatted at the table, I realised he was an old colleague from my mid-30s when I worked as a chef. He seemed like a sensitive soul, and we enjoyed reminiscing about our old workplace.

We met several times at these group events and became friends. He asked for my number and invited me out for dinner. Our relationship grew, and we bonded over our shared love for baking and dining out.

However, things took a turn when he went on a solo trip to Thailand. He frequently video called me during his trip, exhibiting signs of obsession and neediness. I couldn't shake the feeling that he might explore the darker aspects of Thailand known for British men visiting bars and strip clubs.

Upon his return, he confessed to wild nights of drinking with English friends. Despite my suspicions, I continued to date him as he showered me with gifts and nice meals.

One day, I felt compelled to check his phone while he left it beside me on the sofa as curiosity got the better of me. To my dismay, I discovered he was a member of PornHub, which angered me deeply.

So teach us to number our days, that we

may apply our hearts unto wisdom.

Psalm 90:12 (KJV)

God does not want us to rush into things; to be prudent in our actions, as we reap what we sow. I allowed more pain into my life than needed because I was desperate for love and acceptance from man. If I had not been, things would have been very different. I confronted him about it, and he denied it. I took screenshots of his favourite videos and showed them to him. He fell over in shock and begged me, denying he was on the site. He said he would not look at them again. He was full of lies, embarrassment, and fear of losing me.

And if thy right eye offend thee, pluck it out, and cast it from thee: for it is profitable for thee that one of thy members should perish, and not that thy whole body should be cast into hell. And if thy right hand offend thee, cut it off, and cast it from thee: for it is profitable for thee that one of thy members should perish, and not that thy whole body

should be cast into hell. Matthew 5:29-30 (KJV)

We carried on as normal, not addressing the issue, just trying to enjoy the life we had.

Months went by, and I found myself repeating the same actions. I checked his mobile and discovered more videos. Additionally, at his home, he opened his laptop one day in front of me, and a porn site icon was visible. I could see the awkwardness on his face as he quickly shut it down.

God's ways are wise and true; they prevent pain and suffering.

A prudent man foreseeth the evil, and hideth himself; but the simple pass on, and are punished. Proverbs 27:12 (KJV)

Therefore shall a man leave his father and his mother, and shall cleave unto his wife: and they shall be one flesh. Genesis 2:24 (KJV)

Nevertheless, to avoid fornication, let every man have his own wife, and let

every woman have her own husband.
1 Corinthians 7:2 (KJV)

I saw it that seeking satisfaction elsewhere was akin to cheating for me. Therefore, I believed I deserved fidelity and loyalty, leaving anyone who didn't respect my commitment. I remained faithful and expected the same.

Throughout this relationship, I repeatedly addressed the issue with him. Being a sensitive person, he was generally okay except for this aspect. I explained my aversion to pornography, emphasising its harmful effects on women, children, and even men, deeming it as evil.

The breaking point in our relationship occurred when I was attacked by the demons afflicting him. He recounted waking up to a heavy sensation on his chest, with something breathing down his ear, even hearing what sounded like a heartbeat or similar.

I found out about this incident when he messaged me about it in December 2018. We exchanged emails, and I urged him to pray to

Archangel Michael. Here are his actual words.

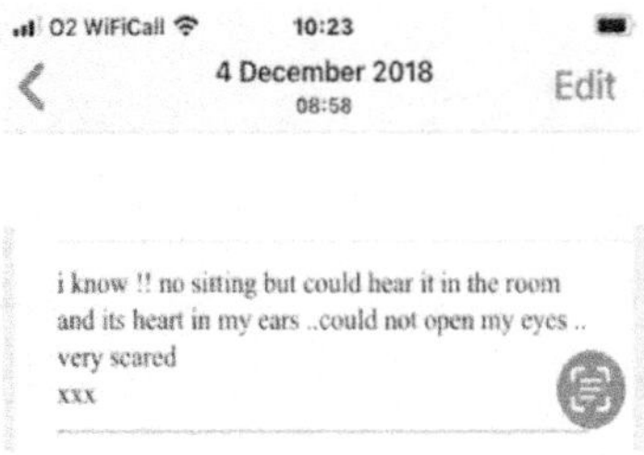

This was proof of the true manifestation of demons. He had opened doors to the devil through the spirit of lust. His life was in disarray; he hated his job and constantly cursed himself, expressing feelings of inadequacy and worthlessness.

I attempted to help him through prayer and by showing him the consequences of his actions, but he remained stubborn, deceitful, and attached to his sinful ways.

The last time I spent time with him, I found scratches on my arm afterward, leaving me in shock and fear. I had to pray earnestly for protection. See the image below.

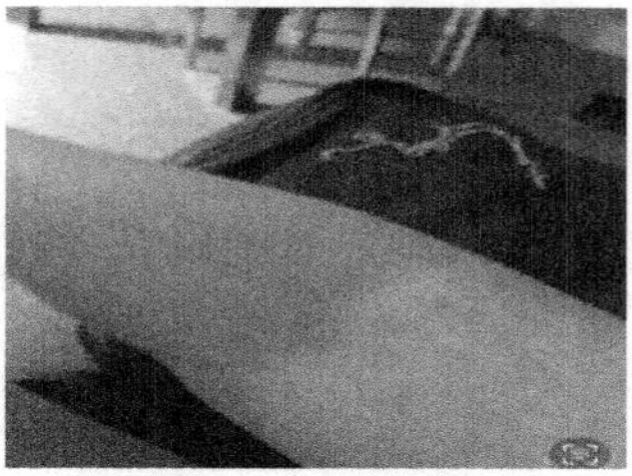

The law of the Lord is perfect, converting the soul: the testimony of the Lord is sure, making wise the simple. Psalm 19:7 (KJV)

I was seeing that most men were living like this; they were in the world, caught in this trap of perversion. In fact, he said to me, "all men watch pornography." Why was I so naïve to this fact? Men who were not following Christ were dead in their sin. I was looking forward to some peace and time alone, to recover, love myself, and embrace single life. I was to learn, via hardships, pain, and suffering, who I was.

After my last relationship and my salvation, the Lord said to me, "I HAVE NOTHING IN COMMON WITH MAN." Wow, that really hit my spirit.

Concerning the works of men, By the word of Your lips, I have kept away from the paths of the destroyer. Psalm 17:4 (NKJV)

So basically, he was saying that my own ways caused me suffering, and he did not want that for me and Man was the destroyer.

Chapter 10

Around In Circles

Years of listening to Satan had me going from one thing to the next. I had the spirit of error in me. It had a stronghold, making the same mistakes and not learning from them was my problem. I failed myself by not noticing my own ways and storing up wrath for myself with God. Believing there was someone out there who would be the one for me was because I had worldliness in me, not in the Spirit, His presence. The spirit of rejection also had a stronghold in me; it was a hopeless situation. It seemed like I had zero self-control, which is a fruit of the spirit. I was demonically oppressed and possessed by demons. I realised after my salvation that I had a spirit of lust as well, as I was fornicating by looking for a relationship outside of marriage, doing things my way, not God's way. God's way is perfect.

I had so many different jobs trying to make ends meet, but I preferred to stay away from people, not knowing why I isolated myself and kept away from the noise outside. I had lost my faith in people big time. Sometimes I would start something, a new venture, a new business idea would come up, and then it would lead to nothing. So much wasted time and money; I was truly lost.

I was having so many mind battles; it was untrue. I was struggling to stay centered and focus on anything. I knew something was off. Satan was having a field day with me. I never knew how strategic Satan was; most things that happened to me in my early years were planned to destroy me, take me out. I know a part of being a Christian is long-suffering, but my suffering had been at another level. I wonder how I overcame it. And I was not a Christian. Christened at birth made me think I was a Christian, but I had no idea what it meant to pick up my cross and follow Jesus. Oh, how I wish I knew Jesus when I was young.

Put on the whole armour of God, that ye may be able to stand against the wiles of the devil. Ephesians 6:11 (KJV)

I also never knew that life was spiritual and to overcome it, I needed the Word of God. Most things were demons or attacks from Satan's kingdom. I only used to focus on heavenly beings like Angels. But even Satan disguised himself as an Angel of Light. The Bible says, "Resist the Devil, and he will flee from you."

Submit yourselves therefore to God. Resist the devil, and he will flee from you. James 4:7 (KJV)

How can you resist what you don't know about? I was later told that I am an overcomer. I was being pruned big time by God; they say whom God loves, he will chastise. I never knew what was happening spiritually at the time; I just knew it was painful. Pruning often happens during our trials because suffering is a prime time for the revelation of the idols in our hearts.

My brethren, count it all joy when ye fall into divers temptations; Knowing this, that the trying of your faith worketh patience. But let patience have her perfect work, that ye may be perfect and entire, wanting nothing. James 1:2-4 (KJV)

Despite facing adversaries, I remained steadfast. Rather than retaliating, I chose to maintain my composure, refraining from speaking ill of others or seeking revenge. It was not in my nature to harm or slander anyone, and I am grateful to God for granting me such wisdom. Amen.

Be not overcome of evil, but overcome evil with good. Romans 12:21 (KJV)

Therefore all things whatsoever ye would that men should do to you, do ye even so to them: for this is the

**law and the prophets.
Matthew 7:12. (KJV)**

Be not deceived; God is not mocked: for whatsoever a man soweth, that shall he also reap. Galatians 6:7 (KJV)

Chapter 11

Rescued Set Free

One day, I was at home, essentially sitting in my house, doing the usual things we do, and not really wanting to venture out much, just trying to earn some money to pay my bills. Yeah. I felt very trapped and realised that I didn't want to continue like this. I just wanted to escape from it all, as I didn't like the situation. I began reciting a prayer I discovered, Let me share with you exactly what I prayed.

"I affirm that God has seated me with Christ Jesus in the heavenly realms, far above all principalities and supernatural powers of

darkness. I now command all wicked spirits to cease their work and be bound in the presence of the Lord Jesus Christ. I also bind all wicked spirits assigned to rebuild evicted spirits' strongholds. They may not do that! I forbid any transference of spirits dividing, restructuring, or multiplying wicked spirits working against me in the name of Jesus."

Well, this was the prayer that was to set me free but I didn't know what was gonna happen after this. It was amazing. and I started praying out over me in my home quite a few times, not knowing that God was hearing this. So one day in March 2020, it was the beginning of COVID. Things were slowing down for me financially. Work was not coming in. And I started to get panicky about it. I was in this job, doing psychic readings, and I was trapped and I knew it wasn't right in my spirit and I wanted a way out but didn't know how to get out. I tried to get a job with an agency. I sent my CV to them. And because of my age, I felt it was against me and they never even came back to me to offer me work. I was sitting at home really stuck with no way out like a bird trapped in a cage. That's the only way I could explain it.

I did eventually get a little job. And it was in a nursery with children. I had this job for about three months. I was very happy to be away from my home and doing something different. Obviously, I hadn't been saved at that point, or repented of my sins. One day at this job. I was sitting with the children while they were playing. I just closed my eyes for a few minutes. And I don't know why I did but I just closed my eyes just to kind of relax myself a bit. Then someone reported me for doing that and I was sacked from the job. Within three months I found myself back at home in the same situation that was trying to get away from Satan had got me back where I trying to get out of basically is trying to make sure I was back there again still trapped. So I was feeling really upset and I thought what am I going to do carrying on I had no choice have to continue this work and feed myself. The only way I could feed myself.

Then one day, out of the blue, I was watching a lady on a YouTube video. This lady used to be in the world, teaching New Age teachings, and was a millionaire from her teachings. She was deeply into deception. She had been saved by Jesus and was talking about it. She started talking about Deuteronomy 18:10 – 14 (KJV) below.

There shall not be found among you any one that maketh his son or his daughter to pass through the fire, or that useth divination, or an observer of times, or an enchanter, or a witch. Or a charmer, or a consulter with familiar spirits, or a wizard, or a necromancer. For all that do these things are an abomination unto the Lord: and because of these abominations the Lord thy God doth drive them out from before thee. Thou shalt be perfect with the Lord thy God. For these nations, which thou shalt possess, hearkened unto observers of times, and unto diviners: but as for thee, the Lord thy God hath not suffered thee so to do.

So at that point, I felt deeply convicted and

frightened that I was in the wrong. I was terrified and didn't know what to do. As soon as I read that passage and heard those words, "the Word of God is alive and active," it struck me profoundly. It resonated within me, and I became acutely aware of my wrongdoing. The conviction I felt was intense. Yet, here she was, saved from all of that. And now, I needed salvation or some intervention. Fear overwhelmed me, and I immediately ceased what I was doing. I began to panic. How would I sustain myself? What was I going to do? I continued to pray to the angels and to God, crying out for help.

Then, one day in March 2020, the power of God came over me, and He broke the chains. I felt weird. It was as if I was freed from something, and I started to pray. I felt like I died that day. I can't describe this moment; it's like my spirit died. I just felt dead, but I also felt good. What was going on? I felt dead; what is happening? I thought, should I plan my funeral? I was set free. There was something that I felt free from. At the time, I didn't know what I was free from, but obviously, I was being freed from the chains that the enemy had put around me. Demonic chains, the suppression, the possession of the devil, was broken off of me, basically that day, in my home. It was the most supernatural, unbelievable experience that any human can experience: to be delivered from Satan's clutches.

Later on, I found out that deliverance had taken place in my home, alongside the baptism of fire with the Holy Ghost. I was set free, and where the Spirit of the Lord is, there is freedom. My crying out to God had worked; it set me free.

The same Spirit that had resurrected Jesus Christ from the dead had killed my flesh. It was a quickening; the chains had been broken, unclean spirits were gone, hallelujah. God is powerful, and He does hear us when we cry out to Him. I had to die to myself, and that happened that day; I died to myself.

For Christ also hath once suffered for sins, the just for the unjust, that he might bring us to God, being put to death in the flesh, but

quickened by the Spirit:

1 Peter 3:18 (KJV)

Praise for Deliverance

7 I will tell of the Lord's unfailing love and praise Him for all He has done. I will rejoice in His great goodness to Israel, granted according to His mercy and love.
8 He said, "They are my very own people. Surely they will not betray me again." And He became their Saviour.
9 In all their suffering, He also suffered, and He personally rescued them. In His love and mercy, He redeemed them, lifting them up and carrying them through all the years.

Isaiah 63:7-9 (NLT)

So the Spirit of God fell on me and set me free; Jesus came to set the captives free, and indeed, He does. I was liberated from demonic oppression and possession, and my life has never been the same. I'm a new creation in Christ. After this happened on that day, I picked up the telephone and called a vicar. I started asking the vicar to pray for me and told him what had happened. He prayed for me several times over the telephone and guided me as to what to do next.

Within hours of me letting go of this and realising what happens supernaturally, a huge snake came to my face in the spirit. The serpent's face was literally coming at me with its mouth wide open. Well, I actually hate snakes and I've always hated snakes. I was petrified and I rang a guy who had also recently come to Christ and was experiencing similar things as me. He told me to buy a Bible, so I did. At last, I had the truth. Since I got the word of God, I was on my way to more freedom. I started learning scripture, diving deep into the Word of God. I could not get enough of His Word. I meditated on it day and night. The Bible still stayed with me wherever I went. He was starting to talk to me via the rhema word in the Bible. Verses were jumping out at me, and I was connected to the Lord, my Saviour, at last. Satan continued to attack me in my bedroom, in my dreams, trying to scare me. He had been defeated. Satan was angry. He had lost the fight for my soul. I was free. I had weeks of attacks, and I was fearful. I was guided on Spiritual Warfare by people on the internet.

The next thing, I had no food to feed myself and didn't know what to do. I had no money coming into my home, so I started getting food from charities, going to food banks. My daughter also helped me out with food. I didn't know what to do, but some people were helping me. I was receiving grants from the government as well, a bit of money here and there, so I did not go hungry. God is faithful.

I had to destroy all the idols I had in my home. I went out to make a huge bonfire in the woods. What joy that brought me to destroy all the cards that I had, the oracle cards guiding my life into destruction. I couldn't wait. Any book I had on New Age practices, bought from this New Age teacher, was destroyed. They were all set ablaze in the bonfire, and it was such a wonderful moment to destroy that part of me - that part of me that was obviously a disobedient child, not knowing anything about God, only knowing that there was a God. I has happy to be free from all this, as I wanted to be set free but did not know how it was going to happen. I was still scared because the enemy was attacking me, but I kept praying and eventually, he stopped. I was getting stronger in the spirit. Then the Lord blessed me financially out of the blue. He gave me what I never deserved. God is merciful. God is graceful.

The righteous cry, and the Lord heareth, and delivereth them out of all their troubles.

Psalm 34:17 (KJV)

He revealed the word "grace" to me in my mind, which brought me great joy. It appeared in my inner vision, and seeing the word "grace" reminded me of His grace. He is a gracious Father, full of mercy and love. Once those unclean spirits had departed, I could be filled, though it didn't happen immediately.

And we know that all things work together for

good to them that love God, to them who are the called according to his purpose.

Romans 8:28 (KJV)

The ropes of death entangled me; floods of destruction swept over me. The grave wrapped its ropes around me; death laid a trap in my path. Psalm 18:4-5 (NLT)

He reached down from heaven and rescued me; he drew me out of deep waters.

Psalm 18:16 (NLT)

He led me to a place of safety; he rescued me because he delights in me. The Lord rewarded me for doing right; he restored me because of my innocence.

Psalm 18:19-20 (NLT)

He guided me to a place of safety. Subsequently, I relocated to a more suitable home and settled in. As I adjusted to my new abode, I began experiencing more occurrences with the Lord.

Chapter 12

Overcoming Church Hurt

I realised something about my mindset: I had a spirit of idealism. I was looking for the perfect place to live, the perfect love from people, and perfect life situations. However, nothing was how I had hoped it would be; it all seemed empty. Where did this come from? I was dreaming of perfection in people and myself. Lofty, grand ideas that were unrealistic. I was called a dreamer – my head was in the clouds for sure. Perhaps I was striving to find perfection in the earthly realm. Oh, how naïve I was, and I had to repent of it later on.

Only then did I fully comprehend that the world

was far from perfect, and we are all on a journey to evolve and grow spiritually – to become better people, to love each other, and to have harmonious relationships with our fellow beings. Just as God said to the Earth, "Earth, bring forth fruit," so He says to the life of Jesus Christ in every one of us who knows Him, "Bring forth fruit." The only thing that makes the fruit possible is the fact that there is life from Christ within.

I was not finding the peace and harmony I desired, but then the Lord reminded me of this scripture:

John 16:33 (NIV) - *I have told you these things, so that in me you may have peace. In this world, you will have trouble. But take heart! I have overcome the world.*

I know there are some positive traits of an idealistic mind. I knew I was deeply caring and wanted to see change. I knew I had a gentle heart that was easily offended by harshness and critical words. My sensitivity was quite hard to live with.

Things are not perfect, as we are fallen and sinful in our fleshly nature. We are not in the spirit until we are saved and born again, and then we can strive to be perfected by God's word, evolve further, and deny ourselves.

I could not quite understand why people were not nice to each other. Then I found out it was the spirit in them making them act that way. The blinkers were taken off after I realised that demons were operating in people's spirits – demons of anger, jealousy, pride, perversion, envy, bitterness, unforgiveness, etc. Even I had worldliness in my spirit, chasing after worldly things that do not feed the soul. I knew I was not perfect either.

Satan is very strategic in who he brings into your path to destroy you! If only I had known the Word and his plans, my life might have been different. But, sadly, my story is one of pain, hurt, torment, and much trauma.

When I first went into a church, I was nervous, broken, and in need of prayer and support. I had expectations of meeting kind, loving, and helpful people who would comfort me and help me find the love and comfort I needed after all the warfare I had been through. I tried an Anglican church, then Pentecostal.

I was drawn to Charismatic Christianity because I was being awakened by the Holy Spirit, particularly in the gift of prophecy via dreams and visions from God after the baptism of the Holy Ghost. I then realised that the gifts God had originally planned for me in the womb were finally starting to manifest. I had a dream of oil being poured over me – the anointing oil.

Jeremiah 1:5 (NIV)

"Before I formed you in the womb I knew you,
before you were born I set you apart;
I appointed you as a prophet to the nations."

At church, I was met with strange looks. Some people would cross their arms over their bodies as if to defend themselves from me. I felt uncomfortable and was not received very well. I asked myself why.

I was perplexed – they were church people; surely they were going to receive me and welcome me.

But no, I got such bad looks from some that I went home and felt uneasy in my spirit. I thought the enemy was feeding them with thoughts of my past sins, and they were judging me. Some I met would not even say hello to me in the street when I saw them outside of the church. I recall one man with whom I attended Bible study totally ignoring me in the street after I said hello!

I was deeply discouraged. "Where is the love?" I asked myself.

When they kept on questioning him, he straightened up and said to them, "Let any one of you who is without sin be the first to throw a stone at her." **John 8:7 (NIV)**

The religious leaders continued to question Jesus.

I thought the church would be the place to be around like-minded people of one accord and full of love. So I started to go from church to church, getting the same cold reception. Then I had a revelation that the Lord's spirit was upon me, and it was this they were perceiving. Some people would step back from me and feel uncomfortable when I was in their space. Even my family were cowering and putting their heads down; my neighbours were snarling at me, their faces grimacing when I met them!

I remembered that Jesus was hated as well, by the Pharisees. "What is going on?" I said to myself. People were acting strangely towards me, which highlighted the spirit of rejection I was born with. I was allowing this demonic spirit to have its way. I was still in need of deliverance and had to come out of agreement with this spirit, as the enemy wants me to be isolated and alone so he can bring me sadness and loneliness.

Luke 4:18 (NIV)

18 "The Spirit of the Lord is on me,
because he has anointed me
to proclaim good news to the poor.
He has sent me to proclaim freedom for the

prisoners and recovery of sight for the blind, to set the oppressed free.

I certainly felt strong in my spirit to do the will of God in the area of evangelism. I talked about Jesus to everyone I met; it was as if I were obsessed with Jesus. I was full of the Holy Spirit and could not quench the fire burning inside me to save the lost. I wanted to do outreach; it was burning in my spirit to preach the Gospel to people outside the church.

Matthew 5:6 (NIV)
Blessed are those who hunger and thirst after righteousness, for they shall be filled.

I was alive in Christ, hallelujah. One man at church said he saw a Glory Cloud above me. I also perceived that some were Pharisees – religious people who were attending church but perhaps were not operating in the love of Christ. As I never truly met Jesus at church, some were kind, while others were not. The four walls are not the church; we are.

Acts 7:48 (NIV) "However, the Most High does not live in houses made by human hands. As the prophet says:

Then, at another place, I experienced intimidation, accusations, and gossip. When I walked away, feeling the need to protect myself, I was told I needed to repent for being self-centred. The attackers were relentless.

I actually have a servant's heart; I know my own heart. I even worked in care environments, helping the sick and needy throughout my career. If that is not serving, then what is? The enemy was even using Christians to scatter the flock.

Psalm 133:1-2 (NIV)
How wonderful and pleasant it is
when brothers live together in harmony!
For harmony is as precious as the anointing oil

I was craving harmony and peace with others and not finding it. Some were like wolves in sheep's clothing. One day, I went home and sat down like Elijah, weeping, and I said, "Lord, I've had enough;

I really have had enough."

Perhaps the Lord was teaching me a lesson on forgiving our brothers and sisters in Christ. But I missed the lesson; I don't know – it was all overwhelming. I also had to realise that people in church are still in need of healing and help from their own trauma, just like me, and that some of us have wounds that need healing, so I had a lot to learn.

I was at home some weeks later and had a dream: "Go to church and fellowship." I did just that after praying, and I sought out a church with more warm-hearted Christians, stopping my search for my version of church and instead looking for the real version.

I had to remind myself that we are all battling sin and the flesh and needed to repent. The Lord is merciful and full of forgiveness; this journey is one of repentance and finding peace within a broken world.

Chapter 13

Purpose In The Pain

I had a Damascus Road miracle and was saved – all the glory goes to God. The same Jesus Christ who died on the cross is alive today, unchanging from yesterday to today.

And the Lord shall deliver me from every evil work, and will preserve me unto his heavenly kingdom: to whom be glory for ever and ever.

2 Timothy 4:18 (KJV)

Now that God had saved me, what was next?

Moreover the law entered, that the offence might abound. But where sin abounded, grace

did much more abound: That as sin hath reigned unto death, even so might grace reign through righteousness unto eternal life by Jesus Christ our Lord.

Romans 5:20-21 (KJV)

But as for you, ye thought evil against me; but God meant it unto good, to bring to pass, as it is this day, to save much people alive.

Genesis 50:20 (KJV)

I had a prophetic word spoken over me about saving people trapped in pornography. It was indeed God's will in my life as I battled this invading spirit within my marriage. Familiar spirits are behind the seducing spirits, all part of Satan's plan to lead men and women away from God. The world is rife with internet pornography, invading the minds of many and establishing strongholds. It's a real epidemic in society. Websites containing pornography were among the most visited during the COVID pandemic lockdown.

The term "lockdown" is quite apt, as men and

women were locked in sin, and their lives were spiralling downward toward the pits of hell, metaphorically speaking. I wasn't sure what to do next, but then something supernatural happened.

After weeks of crying, experiencing godly repentance, and battling shame and grief, the Lord gave me revelations about the angels who had been by my side during my early years in London and with the stalker who had sought to harm me. A flood of revelations about my past and why certain events had occurred came to me. He gave me insight into my whole life story.

I have declared, and have saved, and I have shewed, when there was no strange god among you: therefore ye are my witnesses, saith the Lord, that I am God. Yea, before the day was I am he; and there is none that can deliver out of my hand: I will work, and who shall let it?
Isaiah 43:12-13 (KJV)

I was looking for a baptism place and contacted The Last Reformation, who had a map of

Christians conducting baptisms. I was baptised in the sea at Portsmouth in September 2020, and then I was prayed over to receive the Holy Spirit.

Receiving the Holy Spirit:

One morning, I woke up in my bed feeling very alive but uncomfortable, as if I were in the wrong place. During my sleep, my spirit had an infilling of the Holy Spirit. I felt uncomfortable, as if my spirit were in the earthly realm's atmosphere, but my spirit was in heavenly places, seated with Christ Jesus.

It was very uncomfortable, almost painful, to be in this dense atmosphere. I was seeing, feeling, and hearing everything intensely; all my senses were on fire. I wished not to be so sensitive in the spirit. I was filled with the fear of the Lord as well, which was remarkable. The Spirit of God was upon me; it was truly supernatural.

The Spirit of the Lord is upon me, because he hath anointed me to preach the gospel to the poor; he hath sent me to heal the

brokenhearted, to preach deliverance to the captives, and recovering of sight to the blind, to set at liberty them that are bruised.

Luke 4:18 (KJV)

I noticed that my eyes and ears needed protection; my gates needed guarding. It was hard to watch secular TV or anything worldly. One day, while I was out around a swimming pool, I saw people drunk and kissing, and it made me feel weird. I sensed His holy presence strongly that day.

Soon after, I began to be really on fire for the things of God. I started evangelising and winning souls through outreaches. All I cared about was for people to know Jesus. It was an unquenchable fire to save the lost, as I once was lost in the world, and many are still in need of saving.

Jesus was so close; I began having dreams of climbing ladders, like Jacob in the book of Genesis 28:10-17. God was in my place. Jesus would come to me in dreams, and I was becoming very prophetic. He would warn me of things, and I would start praying against them.

I received a revelation about generational curses and embarked on a three-day fast, accompanied by midnight prayers. It became clear to me that sins had been committed against God by my family lineage, extending back three generations.

Thou shalt not bow down thyself to them, nor serve them: for I the Lord thy God am a jealous God, visiting the iniquity of the fathers upon the children unto the third and fourth generation of them that hate me; And shewing mercy unto thousands of them that love me, and keep my commandments.

Exodus 20:5-6 (KJV)

I also knew that my father's house was the reason for the curses. He had many gods in his house, including statues of Roman emperors, goddesses, Egyptian paintings, and busts of various deities. One night, as I prayed to be delivered from ancestral contracts and agreements, and to be delivered from my father's house, I soon visited his home and saw one of the statues with no head. The head was lying on the floor in the garden. I was in awe of how God may have broken the statue through warfare prayer.

Another night, before going to sleep, Jesus stood before my bed. I was both afraid and in awe. It was an open vision. He wore a white robe with a red sash around his waist. He was awesome and majestic, and I sensed his holy presence. He looked at me with a smile, and it made me feel loved. I was beginning to understand visions and dreams more and more, and how God communicates with us.

I later told my father about my encounters with God and how I was baptised. He was under oppression from his wife, who ruled him. He expressed his desire to be baptised, stating that he would ask his wife for permission. I reminded him that he didn't need permission to be baptised; it was his choice. He agreed and made arrangements to be baptised in secret at his home. On the day of his baptism, he wept as he confessed his sinful nature.

He gave his life to Jesus, and I could sense the presence of God in the room. After his confession, he was fully submerged in the water in the bathtub, and we all rejoiced and celebrated Jesus.

I still had more work to do on myself. I needed healing from all the witchcraft that had been done on me. I had several health issues, but I put my trust in God. The Lord said to me, "My grace is sufficient for you." Like Paul, who had a thorn in his flesh, a messenger from Satan, God's grace was sufficient for me. When I am weak, He is strong.

Soon after my salvation, I started praying for my family, asking God to save my daughter and my family. One Saturday, my daughter called me, asking me to go to her home quickly. When I arrived, she told me that a light had come into her home from the lounge window while she was sitting on the sofa. She was shivering and crying during this experience, and she said she saw the name Jesus. We watched the movie "The Greatest Story Ever Told" together, and afterward, she expressed her belief in Jesus. Three of us had been saved at this point, and I was excited for what God was going to do next.

I had a dream about writing a book, and scripture confirmed this calling. I wondered where God was taking me next. I knew I had to submit and stay humble in this process. Some weeks later, the Lord awakened me with Psalm 45 in my mind. I went to read it right away, feeling it was a word for me that my time had come to do His will.

Thou lovest righteousness, and hatest wickedness: therefore God, thy God, hath anointed thee with the oil of gladness above thy fellows. Psalm 45:7 (KJV)

I was now walking closely with the Lord, and He showed me an outward sign of His presence. One day, as I walked down the street with tracts in my hand, a photo was taken, revealing a cross prominently displayed on my back. Within that cross appeared a rainbow – a symbol of God's faithfulness.

For ye shall not go out with haste, nor go by flight: for the Lord will go before you; and the God of Israel will be your reward.
Isaiah 52:12 (KJV)

I was ensnared and trapped as I followed the prince of the air, but God set me free. Amen and hallelujah! I serve a powerful God.

I spent three years in the wilderness, isolated for a reason and equipped for His glory, denying myself and spending time with the Lord. It was tough; all my faults and pride were tested in this place.

I felt overwhelmed and wanted to give up. I had

had enough of this world and wanted to be with the Lord. But there is more to come; it is just the beginning in God's eyes. I questioned everything, puzzled and perplexed. But from God's perspective, it is His will as He reveals His perfect plan. I humble myself for His work. Glory be to God!

And we know that all things work together for good to them that love God, to them who are the called according to his purpose. Romans 8:28 (NKJV)

And they overcame him by the blood of the Lamb, and by the word of their testimony; and they loved not their lives unto the death. Revelation 12:11 (NKJV)

I believe my life holds a greater purpose; I am not here by chance. Chosen, appointed, and anointed by God, I declare my love for you, Jesus. If you, too, seek peace, deliverance, and freedom, join me in this prayer to accept Jesus as your Saviour.

Salvation Prayer (Say this prayer out loud)

Father, I am a sinner in need of Your forgiveness. I ask You to forgive me of all my sins in Jesus' name. I repent and turn from sinning and doing wrong, right now. I believe that Jesus died and rose again for my sin, and I accept His payment. Jesus, I ask You to come into my heart right now and be my Lord and Saviour. Fill me with the Holy Spirit. I thank You, Lord, for hearing my prayer and coming into my heart and saving me according to Your word. I love You, Lord, and I ask You to seal me in the blood of Jesus and help me to live for You all the days of my life. In Jesus' name, Amen.

For I am persuaded that neither death nor life, nor angels nor principalities nor powers, nor things present nor things to come, nor height nor depth, nor any other created thing, shall be able to separate us from the love of God which is in Christ Jesus our Lord.

Romans 8:38-39 (NKJV)

Further scripture reading:

- Hebrews 11:1

- 1 Corinthians 15:1-5
- Matthew 22:34-40
- Galatians 5:22-23
- Psalm 66

As a born-again believer, I can now understand by faith these things:

- I was purchased at a great price.
- I love the Lord Jesus Christ and must walk in obedience.
- I am chosen for such a time as this.
- All the torture and pain Jesus went through was for my healing and salvation from eternal damnation.
- I have a right to all of God's blessings, discernment, and provision.
- My strength is from the Lord.
- No weapon formed against me shall prosper.
- My fruit comes from His Spirit; nothing is from me.

- I am new and do not live by my past; it is forgiven.
- I have happiness and belong to my Father in Heaven.
- I have authority in Heaven to bind things on earth.
- I walk by faith, not by sight.

Statement of Faith:

The Word of Jesus Christ

I believe that the Bible is the Word of God. It is without error in truth and useful for guidance in all aspects of life and ministry. It shows God's way for eternal life in Heaven.

And they overcame him by the blood of the Lamb and by the word of their testimony, and they did not love their lives to the death.

Revelation 12:11 (NKJV)

Printed in Great Britain
by Amazon

62725435R00090